W9-DIV-311

"Pursue perseverance…"

-Apostle Paul

DEDICATION

Many potential world changers with great ideas, talent, good looks, and opportunities nevertheless get nowhere because they give up or change their minds before they get to the goal. This book is dedicated to those who have found a cause worth pursuing to the end and are seeking the will to do it.

You, dear reader, have the potential to change the world for the better.

I dedicate this book to those who will take over the world for good.

CONTENTS

Introduction   Pg 1

1   Grit starts with a real goal   Pg 7

2   Grit faces obstacles squarely   Pg 22

3   Grit believes in miracles   Pg 41

4   Grit believes in something deeper   Pg 53

5   Grit is constantly learning and adapting   Pg 69

6   Grit has partnership   Pg 81

7   Grit has boundaries and self-control   Pg 91

8   Grit is passionate   Pg 103

INTRODUCTION

Several times a week, I like to listen to Ted Talks at Ted.com. Depending on my mood, I listen to authors, leaders, researchers, and adventurers talk about their subjects of interest in about eighteen minutes or less. I love to end my day with it. Something about receiving new information makes my day feel complete, I guess.

One particular day last year, I stumbled on Angela Lee Duckworth's talk about Grit, where she postulates that grit is a better predictor of a student's possible future success than is IQ, or EQ, or any of the other bodies of research that attempt to understand what causes some people to succeed.

She ended her talk with a statement about how we don't know how to teach grit or engender this value in students.

That got my attention. I think people of faith really do have a corner on the value of perseverance, or grit. We believe that good things are possible with persistent belief in the power of God expressed through His chosen delivery system, the action-soaked belief of His created humans. We believe that a person who commits to eternal values will act in certain, extra-intelligent ways because deep down they are committed to the concept that God "is a rewarder of those who diligently seek Him" (Hebrews 11:6). This makes God's people gritty.

Grit is another word for faith.

I don't mean faith as in *I believe in God*, but faith as in *I believe that doing good things produces powerful results, and those results will change the world*.

If one believes there is a God, and that this God is "a rewarder of those that diligently seek Him," then one perseveres in doing good things until results are seen, no matter how hard the interim might be or how big the obstacles are.

We know that IQ is rarely an accurate indicator of whether a person will succeed. We know that people of less-than-desirable backgrounds often become great thinkers, leaders, and world-changers. I think that grit is the true determinant of intelligence. That is, almost anyone who is well motivated can overcome almost any obstacle. The earth is brimming with stories of men and women who had very little education, for example, yet succeeded spectacularly in spite of the same obstacles everybody else had--the same obstacles that caused the rest of us to conclude that it was "just not meant to be." Then highly educated people beat a path to successful people's doors to learn what made them so smart and how to think and act like them.

When people with great motivation set out to do anything, they might at first be measured by their intelligence, past education, family history, looks, or social skills. Such people are questioned constantly about whether or not their work will pay off and whether they are doing something worthwhile.

But gritty people know something that will eventually make them look smarter. They believe that their efforts have their own reward. The universe seems to be instructed to eventually yield

3

to such a soul and wrap itself around that kind of vision.

What causes that kind of person to succeed, to wrap the world around their hearts, and cause much smarter people (as measured by other methods) to eventually come to learn from their seemingly inferior counterparts?

These people have something we all want, but few achieve. It is the quality of grit, built in the laboratory of faith, and motivated by a different value system and different ideas about how the world works.

So what makes up grit, and how can we stir up this mysterious ingredient in our children and in our world? I offer a few ideas toward that end:

Grit starts with a real goal. To be an overcomer of enormous obstacles, we must have a useful end goal in mind that will carry us over the mountains that are in the way and designed to discourage us from the miracle we seek.

Grit faces real obstacles, and faces them squarely. Gritty people do not have an "if it was meant to be, it will be" attitude. Rather, they live in a "if it was meant to be, it will take work" approach to life. They believe that hard work will be rewarded, and that hard workers who keep their eyes on a larger goal will be even more greatly rewarded.

Grit is made up of people who believe in miracles. They do their part and work hard, but they also believe that in some way, God's universe has been instructed to get in on the action when necessary, and that God Himself loves to reward gritty people with amazing disruptions of the usual scientific and societal structure, to help them achieve unusual things.

They learn from the past, from timeless truths, and things that have made sense in every culture for thousands of years. They trust that God has given us insights that we need to know, and that everyone who wishes to learn those insights is welcome into the inner sanctum of God's work and heart.

And gritty people are always learning, always adapting. Instead of lamenting about how things have changed, they are working on understanding how things *could* change, and what has to happen in order to get the job done that they have been called to do. Early achievements do not become platforms of pride, but ways to achieve more and better things in the future.

These people believe in the power of relationships and partnerships. They see how any one person can pull their own weight, but two people dedicated to a common goal can pull as much as five times their own weight. They constantly seek ways to get the job done in larger and more productive ways, leveraging the gifts, ideas, and styles of the people around them for the utmost end value.

And they believe in self-control. One hour of allowing oneself to indulge in a self-destructive thing can bring years and years of pain and diversionary effort to repair the damage. Gritty people know to focus on the prize and avoid harmful distractions.

I believe there is a quality, skill, and attitude in life that trumps all other skills in predicting whether or not people will succeed in whatever they have set out to do.

It is the quality of grit.

Chapter 1
Grit Starts with a Real Goal

"Fight the good fight for the true faith. Hold tightly to the eternal life to which God has called you, which you have confessed so well before many witnesses."

--1 Timothy 6:12, New Living Translation

"I just found out my wife's having an affair."

It's a typical Sunday afternoon for many pastors: comforting broken, hurting people around the altar. I'm looking into the eyes of a man who has been part of our congregation at Freedom Valley Church for several years. The weight of what he's saying forces his head and shoulders down toward the floor.

"I'm so sorry, Ed," I said.

"She's already moved out, living with the other guy," Ed said. "She took the kids."

I nod, listening and hurting with him.

I brace myself for what often comes next. Most people in tough situations need to vent, even complain a little, or talk about how hurt they feel. Some are inexpressibly angry and wanting to lash out at the person who has created such far-reaching pain. It's an understandable urge, and after thirty years of ministry, I know to just listen and guide them through it with prayer and encouragement.

But Ed doesn't vent. And he's not angry, exactly. What he says next is astounding.

"I need prayer for friendliness. I want to be friendly to my wife."

Needless to say, most betrayed spouses are not praying for peace. Many of them want war, or at least a smidge of revenge. This guy wants *friendliness?*

"I think I want my marriage to survive. I want my kids to grow up with parents who love each other. I want to raise them peacefully. I want to be able to forgive each other and move on. So first, I think I need to figure out how to overcome my pain and be friendly in this situation."

I had to hand it to him: he was a man with a plan. Even with his wife in another man's house, with his children, after an infidelity, he was formulating a strategy for making things right. And it started with the smallest, purest step.

We prayed together every Sunday. Weeks went by. Then months. Every week, Ed was there after service to ask for prayer for more friendliness as things developed. While some weeks were harder than others, he never wavered in his faith that she would see his kindness and respond to it…somehow, some way.

Finally, the Sunday came when Ed had good news. "Gerry, she sent me a letter. She said she's sorry and she wants to come home."

"Great!" I said. "That's what we've been praying for!" I tried to speak encouraging words and wondered if he could pick up on my own heart's confusion about the matter.

"Yes," he said, "but it's harder than I thought to welcome her back home. I'm still struggling with some anger."

"Remind me of your big picture," I said. "What's the big win?"

"I want my family back together. I want my kids to grow up in a peaceful home, with happy parents." I could see his eyes looking at it, the total package ahead. He said it like he had already experienced this amazing miracle, a miracle I was still struggling to see at all.

"Then let's focus on that picture together," I told him.

The next Sunday, Ed told me he hadn't let himself think about anything but that ideal future. The more he kept the goal in mind, the more guided his day-to-day steps became, and he could feel himself getting closer and closer. When there was a nasty exchange with his wife, or when he went days without seeing his children, he held onto the ultimate goal, and it steered his behavior toward friendliness. He could do it because he knew it was an important step on the way to his dream.

Eventually, that wife did move back home, as if drawn inexorably to the power of the picture of a happy family that Ed saw. Of course, there was still much healing to be done, and many details to be worked out, but Ed's gritty faith drove him on to find a better place for him and for his family. Every week after our worship experiences, Ed was still waiting to pray with me because a partial answer to his request was not enough. For another year or more, we prayed together almost every Sunday--that he would be able to release his anger, that he would really love her again, that his forgiveness would go deep, and that he would know how to bring healing to his children for what they had to face throughout that separation.

Some people face incredible odds and yet win. The very things that makes other people run away actually motivate them with a can-do spirit. They refuse to back down, refuse to give in, refuse to waver, and they are rewarded for it.

GRIT NEEDS A REASON

Nobody stands up to ridiculous odds unless they have built the reasons inside, and the reasons are strong. They know what the destination looks

11

like, and they want to get there more than anything. In other words, they have built for themselves a real and useful vision for a brighter future.

What I love about Ed's story is that he learned to spend his time daydreaming about what *could* be, instead of focusing on the dreariness or abject painfulness of what was. While his family and friends were telling him to give up, and were bad-mouthing his wife, he chose to put the pain aside and imagine a better scenario. He chose to have faith and trust in the goal that God had put in his heart.

The Biblical story of David and Goliath illustrates the point. David arrives on the scene as the murdering, raping, thieving hordes of Philistines have organized themselves for battle against his people on the opposite hill. A huge behemoth-of-a-man comes out and screams obscenities and mockery, daring them to send somebody, anybody, over to fight him.

Nobody moves. For days David's countrymen whisper about how they should "live to fight another day," and not get rash about how to handle this brutal killer. They talk about how huge his spear is--*larger than a weaver's beam!*-- and they talk about his nine-foot-tall stature. They talk about how he was a man built for war. And they look around at each other, too terrified to do anything.

Until David hears it.

David had recently arrived to bring food and gifts to his older brothers, from their father. Society says he's merely a shepherd boy, not ready for battle.

But David's a different kind of guy. He's cut from a different cloth and hears everything with a different filter.

Goliath comes out yelling again, and all the other soldiers run away. David looks around and asks "So I heard there is a reward for taking this guy down. Can you tell me about the reward?"

"Oh, it's huge!" somebody gushes, as they watch the sorry spectacle of proud fighting men running like cowards while the giant screams his threats. "You get to marry into royalty and be family with the king for life. You and your whole family will never pay taxes again!"

David likes the sound of that. He starts to see a big picture that looks pretty sweet. He asks around some more, confirming the reward, and starts to muster up a crazy dream of defeating the giant, freeing his people from war, and becoming cronies with the king.

Just then one of his older brothers finds him, and just like an older brother, calls his bluff with teasing and bullying.

> *But when David's oldest brother, Eliab, heard David talking to the men, he was angry. "What are you doing around here anyway?" he demanded. "What about those few sheep you're supposed to be taking care of? I know about your pride and deceit. You just want to see the battle!"*

When David presented himself to King Saul, the King concurred, reminding David that he's not cut out for the battle.

GRIT SEES POSSIBILITY

But David sees himself and his people differently. He knows that the enemy's victory would bring every kind of evil into their world, so there is no other option for him! Check out his reply:

> *"I have been taking care of my father's sheep and goats," he said. "When a lion or a bear comes to steal*

14

a lamb from the flock, I go after it with a club and rescue the lamb from its mouth. If the animal turns on me, I catch it by the jaw and club it to death. I have done this to both lions and bears, and I'll do it to this pagan Philistine, too, for he has defied the armies of the living God! The Lord who rescued me from the claws of the lion and the bear will rescue me from this Philistine!"

So many of us are quick to list the ways we're not qualified for the job, but David knew that he had it in him. He reminds himself of the things he's gotten through before, and knows he can do it again.

The king lets him give it a shot and lends David his personal armor and weaponry. It's old and clunky and gets in the way more than anything, so David ditches it. He goes with what he knows: small stones from the nearby stream and his trusty slingshot--not exactly promising.

And then, more trash talk. The world loves to trash talk our dreams, don't they? Look at what Goliath says to David:

"Am I a dog," he roared at David, "that you come at me with a stick?" And he cursed David by the names of his gods.

15

"Come over here, and I'll give your flesh to the birds and wild animals!" Goliath yelled.

David doesn't budge. I love his crazy, bold response.

David replied to the Philistine, "You come to me with sword, spear, and javelin, but I come to you in the name of the Lord of Heaven's Armies—the God of the armies of Israel, whom you have defied. Today the Lord will conquer you, and I will kill you and cut off your head. And then I will give the dead bodies of your men to the birds and wild animals, and the whole world will know that there is a God in Israel! And everyone assembled here will know that the Lord rescues his people, but not with sword and spear. This is the Lord's battle, and he will give you to us!"

Before Goliath can show off his mean combat skills, David gets a running start, rushing toward him and landing a stone dead center in Goliath's forehead, knocking him out.

So the little guy had some skills after all.

To add insult to injury, David walks up and takes Goliath's big sword from his sheath to cut off the giant's head and kill him with his own weapon.

A fairly solid victory.

In my many years of coaching and mentoring young leaders, I've seen what a lack of vision can do to a person. Time and time again, passionate people full of raging potential start strong only to fizzle out. Almost every time, it's a lack of vision. In fact, they often start out with a goal in mind that's maybe a year or two down the road, and once they get there, they suddenly feel broken-down and defeated. When everybody else is ready to throw a party, they're off to the side, exhausted and discouraged. Why? Because their old vision is now complete, and they forgot to come up with a new one to keep them going. Somewhere in the details, they lost sight of the big picture. They turned their lifelong marathon into a two-year sprint, and now they're tired and ready to quit.

Ed was in a similar spot when his wife finally wrote him that apology letter. His dream of his wife responding to his kindness had come true! But now what? As silly as it seems, it's a common stumbling block to feel empty and lost after a victory. Suddenly, there's no vision anymore. Where do we look for the next step? Back to the big picture! When Ed and I remembered it together, he was back on track. We referred to

the big win and found the next step to work
toward.

GRIT'S GOT LOVE

Love is scary and risky. When we really love
something, we have to work up a lot of courage
to come anywhere near it. Think of the middle-
schooler with a crush on a classmate, or the
woman with a beautiful voice before an audition.
Love puts us on pins and needles and requires
vulnerability to see it through. We go out on a
limb for it, and sometimes we get hurt. When
God puts a vision for something beautiful in our
hearts, something we have to run after with love,
it can be terrifying. Gritty people see it through
because they allow themselves to run towards
love without holding back.

The Bible tells us that without vision, we
perish. Gritty people understand the importance
of a grand dream, and they hold onto it through
every phase of the process. They let it inform the
first little step, and each one as they go on.

In Ed's case, his goal was to raise his kids
with their mother, in a peaceful home. The
Goliath of forgiveness, the Goliath of
overcoming offense, is one of the biggest

Goliaths of all, but Ed took a running start, declared his goal, and stuck to it with grit.

Gritty vision, of course, does not do everything. The very nature of vision means that we focus on one thing, ignoring or giving up on everything else! Vision may be as much about admitting that we cannot do everything, as it is about finding that *one* thing we should be doing. It is taking the time to get good at one thing, because getting good at one thing takes time, and every*one* cannot be good at every*thing*! Vision then, can be about choosing which thing we will be good at.

Ed chose his family, being willing to give up a lot of things others achieve, because he decided to go after the gold, build a dynasty, and get good at one thing.

There are so many exciting tools we can take from Ed's story, and from David's. Let's work through them together.

GETTING GRITTY: DEFINING MY GOAL

1. What is the big win for me right now? What does life look like once I've won?

_____

_____

_____

2. The world loves to trash-talk (and we often trash-talk ourselves, too). What are the negative voices saying?

_____

_____

_____

3. What trials have you already come through that prove them wrong? What does God say about you?

_____

_____

4. Like Ed praying for friendliness, what's one small step you can take today?

_____

_____

_____

Pray with me:

> "God, thank you for being my champion, even when others don't see my potential. I choose to see what you see in me. I choose to chase my dreams with grit!"

Chapter 2
Grit Faces Obstacles Squarely

"It is not in the still calm of life…that great characters are formed. The habits of a vigorous mind are formed in contending with difficulties."

--Abigail Adams

It's easy to be distracted these days, maybe more so than ever before. Especially if we *want* to be distracted--because of fear, pain, or just pure laziness--we can usually find a diversion in seconds. When there's a goal weighing heavily on our minds and hearts, it's easy to make excuses in the form of to-do lists. It's tempting to mark things like laundry, email, and other people's business as "urgent," while shrugging away our own calling.

And sometimes it's even blurrier than that. Often we try to get our priorities straight, but then there's a family emergency, or a divorce, or a seemingly insurmountable medical bill, and we feel too far buried, too far behind to keep going. We're ready to call it quits on our calling and just try to survive.

If it's not that, it's our past. We see a shiny, glittering calling up in the clouds, but in reality, we weren't given the skills, we say to ourselves. Our parents weren't good parents. Our school wasn't a good school. Our friends betrayed us. Our government let us down. We're too hurt.

It's hard to face obstacles squarely.

Three years ago, a woman in our congregation came to me with news that stuck in my chest like a dart. A young man in the community had lost his mother and two-year-old daughter in a car accident. His name was Devin, she said, and he was a single dad who loved his daughter more than anything. I didn't know him, but my heart sank into my shoes for him. I felt almost blinded with sadness.

Learning the details of the accident didn't make it easier. Devin's mother, Lisa, had a seizure while driving and swerved head-on into a truck, killing his daughter Jo Anne instantly and taking his mother's life shortly thereafter. A local newspaper reported that little Jo Anne proudly called her grandmother her "best friend."

Unable to get the story out of my mind, I longed to reach out to Devin, to offer him a hug and a shoulder to cry on. My daughter was pregnant with my first grandchild, a girl, and the thought of losing a child was unbearably painful to consider. Finally, when I came across his Facebook profile online, I decided to send him a message. I fumbled for what to say, not knowing him or if this would even be helpful to him, but the Holy Spirit helped me write these words:

Devin,
We have been praying for you a lot today. I heard your daughter and mom were killed in a car accident. I don't know you well but I want you to know we have been praying for you constantly. If I can help, please call me on my cell. I'd love to meet and talk, pray for you, whatever.
Pastor Gerry, Freedom Valley Church

I included my cell phone number and left it at that, not knowing if my words would even reach him, or how they would be received.

I didn't hear back for almost two years.

Then out of nowhere, Devin wrote back the simplest lone sentence:

Hi Gerry, I was wondering if I could come and talk to you sometime?

I was thrilled to hear from him, but also sad and hurting all over again. I couldn't imagine what the past two years had been like for him, without his mother or his daughter.

I wrote back right away and asked if he would like to talk that day. I could meet him at Freedom Valley at 5:45pm. He said he would be there.

I was honored that Devin would trust me with how he was feeling and seeing the world. We met in the church lobby that evening, and he told me how things had gone from bad to worse, how his family was having such a hard time moving on, and how his father hadn't.

His father, Paul, the husband of Lisa and grandfather of Jo Anne, had lost his two greatest treasures in that horrible accident. He and Lisa were married for more than twenty years, and their greatest joy was their grandchildren. Of them all, he was closest with Jo Anne.

After the accident, Paul took to drinking and essentially drank himself to death less than a year later.

Having lost his mother, father, and daughter within eleven months, Devin was broken. Still, I could see the slightest hope in his eyes, and his kindness towards me, a stranger, was striking. I could see that Devin wanted to heal, wanted to figure out how to exchange the pain for something worth living for again. I answered his questions about prayer, God, and church the best I could and told him he was welcome at Freedom Valley any time, and we would love to be there for him, to help him through. I told him that sometimes healing comes through making new relationships and helping others.

Sure enough, Devin started showing up at church, and before long, I was seeing his name on volunteer team sign-up sheets. He was there to get his healing, and he was going after it with his trademark kindhearted perseverance. When

27

asked about his family, he didn't shy away from talking about the accident, or his father, or his emotional struggles. He held up the picture of his daughter with pride and faith that healing was slowly coming for him. He joined the youth ministry team and is still regularly helping teens heal from their own pasts. He is a powerful force of healing for our entire community.

Devin's tenacity--his grit--is astounding to watch. Unlike his dad, for whom the losses were too much, Devin found a way to stand up to the pain and keep going. His bravery is remarkable, and his generosity in helping others is staggering.

Facing obstacles squarely is hard enough in regular, everyday life, but coupled with the pain and grief that many of us have, it can feel impossible. Gritty people find a way.

But how?

Heroes with grit define reality differently. When others look at life and say, "it's too hard," or "you have to cheat to get ahead in this life," gritty people know better.

They see reality as a place with potential, no matter the circumstances. They commit to loving their lives and valuing their experiences, no matter how dark they seem at times. They trust that as long as they are seeking a way, they will find it.

GRIT NIXES EXCUSES

Gritty people don't expect worthwhile things to be easy or to fall into place. Instead of shrugging off obstacles with an "if it was meant to be it will be" attitude, they seem to believe "if it was meant to be, it's worth a lot of hard work."

Nor do they give themselves a pass for growing up in the midst of dysfunction and pain. They don't blame their parents for not raising them right or for damaging them when they were young.

Gritty people know that God is bigger than the pain, the past, and the slim chances of success. They know that excuses waste time, and facing obstacles squarely is the blazing trail to success.

Take Gideon, for example. Gideon is the Biblical hero we meet in chapter six in the book of Judges. His story serves as incredible motivation for anyone who has a messed-up family, grew up in a messed-up culture, and was raised to be part of the problem, not the solution.

But Gideon allowed certain circumstances to change all that.

It all started in a season of great turmoil. Things in his community were careening downhill fast. No one was able to stop the neighboring nations from stealing, oppressing, and causing mayhem. Surrounding hordes of thieves were invading their land, destroying their crops, stealing their livestock, and forcing Gideon's people to scatter and hide in caves in the mountains.

Things were going wildly wrong all over the place, and hope was fading. No one seemed to place the blame where it really was--on a culture killing itself with selfishness, from the inside out, where God had simply stopped protecting them because of their own determined self-destructiveness.

Whenever someone got a little plan and started sowing seeds to raise a crop, the neighboring Midianites would come steal the crop away just as it became ripe for harvest. Israel was reduced to depression. In the midst of cursing the darkness, somebody somewhere started crying out to God again for help.

And God did help, as He always does when asked. His help came in the form of words sent by a prophet. Prophets are simply people who see what God is up to, and declare truth so that it can be received, so that a listing ship can be righted through the declaration of a useful reality.

The prophet reminded them that God had an amazing plan for this nation, and that they had not treasured His plan. He told them they had created their own pain by taking on the customs, attitudes, and sins of other gods, having become like their neighbors, and where they had once raised the average of kindness, goodness, and peace in the neighborhood, now they were dragging that same average down by becoming just like everyone else around them. They weren't being true to who God made them to be, and as is often the result, their identity was in shreds. They were miserable and defenseless.

And God began searching for one gritty guy to rescue his people. He sent an angel with instructions to find someone that He could work with, someone through whom He could show off His power and love for people. He chose an underdog, a nobody, and the least of the least to do it.

It's interesting that when God looked for a future hero, he did not go to the local hangout to find someone who was sitting with his friends lamenting about how bad life had become. Gideon was not hopelessly adding up the reasons why it was not worth the effort to do anything, try anything, or even work to make life better for himself and his family.

Just the opposite. The angel of God went looking for a guy who was hiding--but he was also working and doing his best. Gideon was threshing wheat at the bottom of a winepress to hide from the oppressors. He was working hard, doing what he could in a bad season, from a bad family, at a time when there was a good chance that after a lot of hard work, thieves would steal it all away in the end. Yet he worked on!

And the angel went to him with a message: *I could make you into a mighty hero!*

There was much work to be done first. Gideon thought too many things that were squarely wrong. He was full of ideas that were holding him back and needed to be addressed. He had to be trained to think differently about himself, about his people's history, about how

God works in the world, and about how to move forward.

He started with a valid question. Well, a few questions. "If the Lord is with us, why has all this happened to us? And where are all the miracles our ancestors told us about?"

Good questions, right? Gritty people seem to know something about asking the right questions. For example, I commonly hear angry people mutter something like, "If there was a God and He is good, then why is there so much pain in the world?"

These are powerful questions that, when asked honestly, can lead a person toward some amazing insights.

Gideon's pain, and the pain of His people, were not a result of God's absence, but because God had told them how to avoid pain and they chose to ignore his words! If as a child your mother told you not to go out without a coat because it's cold outside, and you chose to ignore her words and then got very, very cold, it would not prove that your mother was absent, but that you chose to ignore her instructions!

Yet deep in our souls, a certain illogical belief system often takes root and destroys.

GRIT OWNS ITS STRENGTHS

The angel who showed up in Gideon's winepress had started out their encounter by describing life as it really was ("The Lord is with you") and also by calling him by a powerful title-- "mighty man of valor."

What a title! And I'd bet that after giving that title, the angel waited for Gideon's response.

This is my guess because I have tried it often. In watching God work and trying to emulate bits of His wisdom, I often try to call people by great descriptors, then wait.

"You have great potential as a leader."
"You have a brilliant mind."
"I think you are a world changer."
"You have an amazing communicating gift."
"You are beautiful/handsome/talented."

Those with potential to go to an exciting new level usually respond viscerally. It means the world to them that their core potential has been noticed.

Or sometimes they will respond negatively, covering up their vulnerability with sarcasm, doubt, or even outright resistance--but the gut reaction is there. Maybe they have wished that they were those things so deeply that they have resisted any hope in their hearts, in the sad belief that if they could shield themselves from hoping it was true, then they could never disappoint themselves. It's a horrible, backhanded, debilitating belief system designed by an intelligent evil to keep them away from their own potential.

But Gideon's potential to deliver his people from oppressors was useless until he showed grit to overcome the obstacles on the way to his own greatness. And his own beliefs had to be straightened out so that he could find a grit that came from deep, personal faith in the God who would never leave him and who only allowed obstacles in his way as a tool to produce the golden quality of grit.

Gideon's first task was to confront the family that had led his nation in despicable practices, like superstitious child sacrifice and the worship of false gods. He had to face his own fears, risk his own death, recruit an army, and learn how to leverage that army to overcome through their wits rather than brute strength. These things became the center of his new reputation and fame ("might man of valor!"), and all of them required grit.

In chapter twelve of Judges, we read that God put it on Gideon's heart to raise an army. Thousands came, and yet his thousands of soldiers were up against an army so strong it could not even be counted! Astounding every belief of Gideon's own military strategy, God tells him that he has *too many* soldiers, and that he only needs certain ones.

GRIT GETS FOCUSED

And then God tells Gideon how to identify the gritty ones from the rest and how courage overcomes brawn. God instructs Gideon to take all of his soldiers down into the valley to drink water by a stream. Only the ones who drank without taking their eyes off the enemy were gritty enough to win in such a courageous battle plan. Only soldiers who knew how to hold their ground under intense fear and overwhelming odds could endure.

On the given night, Gideon and just 300 men surrounded the enemy's camp, and WON THE BATTLE OVER AN ARMY TOO NUMEROUS TO COUNT.

How did they do it? I am so glad you asked! The *how* of this battle is an object lesson in the indomitable power of unyielding belief in God, in moral rightness, and in the force of character.

There was no way to get a huge army to sneak up on the enemy. And even if it were possible, there were not enough fighting men in all of Israel to face this unbelievable, innumerable, wildly-more-technologically-advanced enemy.

They simply had to find a way to trick them into thinking there was more of them than there really were. They had to find a way to train less of them--only 300--to *act* as if they were people that they were not.

Three hundred men were trained with simple instructions: we are going to sneak into positions around the enemy camp. When the signal is given, each of them was to attack as if they were directing an entire army of troops. In others words, the enemy would need to actually think that there were 300 *armies* coming against them, not 300 men.

And so each man went out with unusual instruments of battle. Each one carried a lit torch that was hidden inside a clay pot until the signal was given. This would provide the needed visual stimuli that would make the enemy see *many* armies. They were also to carry a trumpet, such as the trumpets used by sophisticated armies of their day to direct their troops during a battle. Each general normally had with him a trumpeter who would issue signals to his troops, such as an attack signal, a retreat signal, or other pre-arranged communications.

When the day of battle came, Gideon and his 300 "generals" crept into position, probably crawling on their bellies for the last half mile or so to avoid being heard or seen. When all of them had time to get into position, in the dead of night, Gideon gave the signal.

The enemy, sleeping soundly, thought they heard 300 generals commanding 300 armies. They saw 300 torches suddenly blazing across the night sky and heard 300 armies being given the command to attack. In their intense, sleep-induced confusion, every man started blindly stabbing at whatever form was close to them.

Many died without even knowing *they had killed each other*, facing only 300 men.

Gideon's enemy was too evil, too large, and too oppressive to ignore. Gideon *had* to face the evil. Yet he was hiding till an angel showed up to tell him he was God's answer, that God would carry him through it, and that he would win if he started following God's advice instead of the common wisdom espoused by everybody else.

And he won. Gritty people just do.

GETTING GRITTY: FACING OBSTACLES SQUARELY

1. What distractions am I allowing to take my time and energy when I should be focusing on my calling?

_____

_____

_____

2. What past pains make me feel like I can't do it? What family issues are holding me back?

_____

_____

_____

3. Gritty people know that a few people doing things God's way can trump any army. Who are some strong, faithful people in your life that you can stand together with?

_____

_____

_____

Pray with me:

"God, I repent of allowing distractions and excuses to get in my way of pursuing your call on my life. I ask you to show me the opportunities to pursue, on the way to my dream."

Chapter 3
Grit Believes in Miracles

*"The most incredible thing about miracles
is that they happen."*

--G.K. Chesterton

Gutsy, gritty people look at lousy
circumstances and believe it can be done anyway.
They refuse to be defined by the way things
currently are, because they know they can be
made better.

My friend Brandy has a beautiful mission in

her heart: to help special needs children and adults by teaching them to ride horses.

Believe it or not, people with special needs benefit tremendously from riding horses and often report major improvements in physical, mental, emotional, and social areas of their lives. Brandy's program, Shining Stars, has helped people with all kinds of disabilities to rehabilitate, learn new skills, and gain confidence.

In the 1950s, horseback riding was found to increase mobility in polio patients and since then has grown as a rehabilitation technique for patients with physical disabilities and even learning disabilities. Because the movement of a horse is similar to our own, the horse can actually teach the student about walking and moving in a way that is hard to teach in a classroom. Caring for and guiding the horses is often part of the program too, which can lead to empathy, trust, and other emotional skills.

At Shining Stars, Brandy is often overwhelmed with the need in our community for this kind of therapy. The families she has worked with sing her praises at every opportunity and couldn't imagine life without her program.

But like any program, it takes a lot of work to

keep it going. As the organization grows, they need facilities, volunteers, donations--and horses!

Over the years, Brandy has allowed Freedom Valley Church to take part in the amazing things she's doing. I've been grateful not only to be associated with such an outstanding program, but also to witness Brandy's grit in action.

A few years ago, Brandy came to me with a need for space. There were just too many people that needed help, and she was either renting or borrowing space, or working out of her home, or telling handicapped kids that she simply could not take another student. The families already in the program were needing more, regular help, which required a steady location. And there were always more families pouring in.

It occurred to us that Freedom Valley had space--we had a whole big piece of land behind our church that she could have. It wasn't zoned for it, but with the support of the community, we figured we could get those zoning codes changed and get the money raised to build a riding area right behind the church!

Brandy took on the goal with fierce tenacity. And it was hard work. Getting zoning codes changed is no piece of cake, even with huge support from the community (we once had 200 people pack a town council meeting, each sharing with teary eyes the need for families to have this space). It took a long time just to win that little battle.

After that, reasons for quitting seemed to reveal themselves at every turn. The money wasn't there, the volunteers were too few, the construction plans kept needing to change to appease this detail or that one. We had to add entire parking lots (an expensive and time-consuming venture) before we were allowed to even start building the actual arena. And of course, there was the occasional mean-spirited person who would strike up some kind of controversy around it. And the cost kept going up as regulations came through. It felt relentless.

At Freedom Valley Church, we received a special offering for the arena, our first attempt at raising the nearly half-million dollars we would need to complete the project. It totaled, as I recall, only about three thousand dollars. We were grateful, but it was so tiny compared to what we needed. I thought, *what if we can't do this?*

Not Brandy. She knew that she was doing the Lord's work, that the families who needed this therapy would be served much better inside of that arena, and she knew it was coming. She knew, as gritty people do, that when you do what little you can, God sees it and fills in the rest with a miracle.

We worked on it together for several years, but just couldn't seem to catch a break. Then she had an idea. She put up a sign along the highway that read "Pray for Shining Stars to get an arena!"

It seemed like an odd, small move, but Brandy was listening to that tiny voice inside that said it was important. Gritty people know to listen.

After a few days, a man and woman pulled up to the front of the church and came in to ask about the sign. "We need to move some estate money, and we've been looking for a great, local cause. Can we give you $100,000 for that arena?"

And then they came back later and said they didn't give us enough, and they'd like to give another $50,000.

And then a local foundation contacted us, asking to give $80,000. And the money poured in from places we didn't even know existed. Hundreds of volunteers offered building skills, materials, or what little finances they had to help.

I am very proud to say that my family joined in and helped with this great cause.

And the arena went up.

Today Brandy serves the families at Shining Stars more efficiently and abundantly than ever. She still drives her own beat-up pickup truck with 300,000 miles on it. She's still Brandy. But she made a miracle happen in our town--a miracle of perseverance.

People who have faced incredible odds just seem to get miracles to support their goal. Crazy support comes from unexpected angles and unexpected sources. And these miracles don't even seem to wow the hero of the story. They are, perhaps, expected.

Joshua was that kind of guy. He saw miracle after miracle and seemed to develop understanding, even *expectation* of them. In chapter 10 of his story in the Bible, a good example of his unwavering faith is recounted.

Joshua has forged treaties that did not please God. But Joshua was also a man of his word and lived for a God who was very much of His Word. As a leader, Joshua was expected to honor his commitment to the Gibeonites, even though it was a commitment that should never have been made and came about through deception-- through a lie!

As Joshua is going about his day, he finds out that his lying friends are in trouble. In his usual action orientation to life, he jumps up to help because he had pledged his help when they were in trouble. This was not an easy request and required an all-night march--not an effortless thing to do for people he did not like, respect, or want to befriend. But Joshua had his word to keep, and no excuse was good enough.

When he arrives at the scene of the crime, he jumps on the bad guys using the element of surprise. And God helps by throwing the enemy into confusion. Again, the battle is not easy, and costs him plenty all day long.

GRIT GETS DIRTY

However, amazing things start happening! God sends a hailstorm that helps. Joshua fights on, not willing to sit back and let God do all the work. He believes that what was meant to be would only come to pass by hard work and a serious end goal to make evil stop.

As morning gives way to noon, and noon becomes afternoon, he sees that he is running out of daylight. The coming, inevitable darkness would allow the bad guys to get away and continue their evil ways somewhere else.

The gritty warrior is unwilling to let his investment in this battle slip away. So he does the most logical thing anyone could do. In front of everybody, he boldly looks the sun in the eye and commands it to hold its place as long as he needs it to do so.

And the sun did it.

And Joshua went on with his life.

Isn't it interesting that Joshua totally expected the universe to support him and that His Creator God would make it happen for him?

Gritty people do not see themselves trapped by their circumstances. In the midst of doing all they can and working hard, they believe that God wants them to succeed and that God's creation was built *for* them, not to trap them. They remember that God told humans to "Fill the earth and govern it." (Genesis 1). To *reign over* it! They do not believe that all laws of nature are immutable, because they serve a God that sits *above* the Heavens, and is in charge of it all.

GRIT GETS GUTSY

They believe that miracles happen when God calls for them, and that God loves the requests of his people for those miracles! They believe that "we do not have because we do not ask " (James 4) and that just because something didn't ever happen in history before, that does not mean it can never ever happen! Their relationship with the creator makes them creative and courageous. They approach their heavenly Father like a deeply treasured child would, knowing that God answers prayers like a father, freely saying no if it's not good for them, but loving audacious requests just the same. It turns out that even God is impressed with boldness (see Hebrews 4:16), and encourages humans to exercise it.

People of faith are people who feel fear but nevertheless choose not to respond to what they feel in that case, or let it rule them. Fear is indeed faith, but it is faith in the wrong thing. Fear believes and builds the ideas of defeat and failure, preparing for the worst because it is inevitable, rather than believing that God will help them overcome and live better.

But fear is often first a response that can then become learned and built behavior. When it is overbuilt, it holds us back because it adds up the wrong set of figures and gets a wrong result.

GRIT GETS CREATIVE

Faith-filled believers are not averse to asking God for outrageous interventions because they believe ultimately that we are not more or less than partners with the Creator and that our friendship with Him gives us access to all that He has!

James says, "We do not have because we do not ask God." What might you have if you overcame fear and built faith by asking for great things?

Brandy had to think outside the box to get her therapeutic riding arena. Joshua had to get a little weird to win his battle. Sometimes we make a fool of ourselves for our dreams--and sometimes, God sends miracles to back us up. We have to believe that He will make a way.

GETTING GRITTY: BELIEVING FOR MIRACLES

1. God loves big requests! What are yours?

_____

_____

_____

2. What fears will you need to overcome to move forward with your dreams?

_____

_____

_____

Pray with me:

> "God, thank you for performing big miracles in my life! Teach me to be bolder and braver about trusting you to do the things I can't."

Chapter 4
Grit Believes in Something Deeper

"Why don't you start believing that no matter what you have or haven't done, that your best days are still in front of you ."

--Joel Osteen

I was in a meeting when a reporter showed up at my office asking if I had a moment to answer a few questions. It was one of those eerie moments when the goo of your intuition, normally spread across the cells of your body like light margarine, sucks suddenly together into one tightly packed block that drops heavily into your stomach with a smack. Pay attention, your body tells you. This is no time for protocol. This is important.

Normally I'd have asked her to wait a few minutes until my meeting was over, or in some cases, to make an appointment. But there was this whole heavy-margarine-block thing happening, so I excused myself and followed her into the hallway.

It was loud--unusually loud. Parents and children were chasing one another around for some sort of family gathering, and the reporter and I couldn't get a sentence across. Reluctantly, we stepped outside, where it was pouring rain.

We stood under the front awning, and as she started to ask me questions about some upcoming event, I realized I still couldn't hear her. The thunder was matching her word for word with booming, shattering language. When the thunder would let up for a moment, the pounding rain on the metal roof would drown her out. What crazy cosmic force was keeping this interview from happening, and why was I so intuitively drawn to have this interview right now, when I could so easily put it off? I stared at the soundless woman in bewilderment. It felt like a dream.

The reporter continued to lip-synch, furrowing her brow at my apparent hearing loss and finally gesturing in a way that said, "Let's just do this later."

This is important, the margarine block said. *Pay attention.*

Frustrated and desperate, I turned to the storm and yelled, "I NEED YOU TO CALM DOWN SO I CAN DO THIS!"

And the storm stopped. Immediately. It went silent with the vaguest whimpers, like a scolded puppy.

My ears nearly flopped over dead with happy shock and sweet relief. I turned back to the reporter, whose mouth couldn't seem to close the last half an inch, the modern version of the ancient cartoony *zoinks*.

Zoinks indeed.

She gathered herself quickly, politely ignoring my apparent insanity and/or sorcery, and asked a few questions. I found that she was wondering about my recent CNN interview about the Pentecostal method of prayer called "speaking in tongues." So if she hadn't thought I was weird already, I think I managed to seal the deal.

She got what she needed and left, and I'm not sure which of us was left with a more profound sense of *seriously--what was that?*

But I think it was me.

I don't pretend to understand God, or the weather, or the ways of margarine. These things are beautiful mysteries to me, even after decades of practice and study. What I know is that sometimes the audacity to believe that something huge and wonderful and mysterious out there will occasionally do a guy like me a solid, is all you need.

It was not the first time I'd spoken to the weather. As a little Amish boy I was taught that Jesus spoke to the storm, and the storm settled immediately. I believed in Jesus and loved him. And later, attending a Bible college of a very different faith denomination, I was taught that Jesus wanted us to do all the things that he did. He said we would do all of that and even greater things. I loved his teachings and marveled at the idea of miracles that just plain don't make sense.

So occasionally, I spoke to the weather. Most of the time, it didn't listen, and then once in a while, it would sort of seem to. The expected blizzard, once I demanded it to turn around and dissipate, would sorta kinda do it. Or the rain would come. Or the rain wouldn't come. But it's hard to know whether it was my prayer or somebody else's prayer or anybody's prayer at all.

Out under that awning, with that reporter, it really seemed like it was my prayer.

The amazing thing to me is that it wasn't much of a prayer. It was more like an annoyed outburst, a sassy nip. I didn't quote scripture and consult the higher-ups in my religious circles, or even raise any crucifix paraphernalia, like in the movies. I just couldn't take it anymore, and I cried out what was within me.

It's often this kind of prayer that gets stuff done. I don't pretend to understand it, but I do think there's something profound and beautiful about it. The stuff that doesn't really add up seems to fascinate us the most. I think we're like our Creator in that way. He seems to get a real kick out of watching us just hope we sorta kinda get it enough to try it.

Gritty people get this. Sometimes you just have to believe in something bigger, and let the miraculous mysteries fall where they may.

When you don't know the next step.
When you can't fathom how to get there.
When all is well, and then suddenly, it's not.
When you find out.
When you don't.
When you lose everything.
When you have nothing to lose.

We have to lean on something bigger--some big, beautiful, mysterious cause worth fighting for. Something that makes it worth paying attention to the margarine and the eeriness and the impulse to scream at rainclouds.

GRIT GETS SMART

The little girl in the recent readaptation of *True Grit* reminds me that grit gets smart. She's on the hunt for justice in the case of her father's death, and she shackles herself to the idea. She's constantly quoting the law word for word, reminding herself of the force of justice, the force of the law, and the miraculous occasion when the law bends low and makes things right. She's believing in a concept that some of us have become very jaded about, but she knows that sometimes justice is real, and she believes in the big potential of it becoming realized in her life. That's the kind of crazy faith that gets things done.

Gritty people chase goals that are not just deeply personal or just about themselves. Their grit is not based on a desire to have other people serve them, or for life to become easier for them, or for their own comfort level to rise so they can work fewer hours.

Just the opposite. Tenacious people have developed a goal, or have had a goal thrust upon them, that is larger than they are and has more reason to it than their own comfort. They have found something they are passionate enough about to live *or die* for, but never be neutral about.

And they make it part of themselves. Their goal is their mission, their creed, their mantra. They take the classes and read the books. They memorize the scriptures and quotes. The success stories of their past build their confidence, and they use them like rope to tie their goals to their hearts.

This is why people of faith have an advantage in developing perseverance in the face of obstacles. Their call is not about themselves, their lives are not their own, and their goals did not come from their own daydreams. The intensity of their dreams is something God put within them. It is a cause God created humanity for, and a purpose bigger than their own little lives.

GRIT BELIEVES IN PURPOSE

Purpose is everything.

Some children are told that they come from nothing, that life has no greater meaning than their own experiences, and that they are going nowhere. Those children have been demotivated and are being delivered to the cruelest demons of frustration and self-destructiveness.

The sheer joy of living for something bigger than just me is a generator of the grit that carries a person through the obstacles. A calling, a cause, a purpose that involves the well-being of my people, or the honor of my God--these things produce a motivation that creates grit.

Gritty believers make it their quest to know what God created them for. They want to know the bottom line, and they seek out the root values that God placed within them. Start your quest to find your purpose with a simple prayer to God right now. Ask Him to reveal your mission to you. Knowing what your mission is will add value to your life and give you that vital bounce to your step that will power you through everyday life.

But it is in the tough days that it will matter the most, because that's when you need to know deep down how to get to the center of your soul and focus on your purpose.

Eric Gladhill walked into my life for the first time in May of 1992 at Freedom Valley's very first public worship service. Eric runs an engineering office and is a land surveyor. One Sunday a few years later, he and I were talking about how different our jobs were. Eric suggested that it would be tough to daily be on the helping end of divorce, health problems, funerals, and life challenges of all kinds.

As Eric talked about how tough my job must be, it occurred to me that I thought his job would be equally tough. I doubt if I would last a day at the math, measuring, organizing, managing, planning, and other engineering issues that he had to face. Yet I was born to be a spiritual leader, and I discovered that I loved doing that so very much that I dreamed about doing it for the rest of my life! I guess he felt a little sorry for me to have to do the job I do, and I felt equally sad that he did not get to do it!

I think Eric and I are each operating in the purpose and spiritual gifts that we were born to do, and that creates huge joy in daily life.

In Paul's first letter to the Corinthian church, he tells them that every believer has certain gifts given by the Holy Spirit so that we can help each other. Gritty people know what it is they are gifted with. Every follower of Jesus should find out what their spiritual gifts are, so that when the going gets tough, they know how to dig into the gifts at the core of their being.

You may be interested in a great many things, but a core motivation probably comes from the spiritual gifts that lie at the core of your being. Perhaps God did not give you all of them, because we are built to need each other. I find that most people have two or three gifts that are easily seen and observed by others around them. More are available for the asking, and all of them are available through simply being filled with the Spirit. But all of them are given to you for God to pour through you-- to make the world a better place.

So to find why God created you and put you here, start by asking Him to show you. Then find your spiritual gifts. Study I Corinthians 12 and Romans chapter 12, where the Bible lays out lists of spiritual gifts such as wisdom, special knowledge, great faith, healing, miracles, discernment of spirits, tongues, interpretation, prophesy, serving, teaching, encouragement, giving, mercy, and art. (That last one comes from Exodus 35:31.)

To find your spiritual gifts, you might take a class on the subject or simply meditate on the scriptures mentioned above. Or you could take a free online inventory at spiritualgiftstest.com. Then ask a few trusted friends what they think about your gifts.

When you think you might have found your gifts, try them! In fact, I encourage you to try a lot of things, seeking for what builds that deep inner satisfaction that only comes from following God the best that you can, using the gifts He gave you. As you journey, He will reveal Himself to you and add to your pleasure. Even gritty experiences feel worthwhile and meaningful when we are where God has called us and have confidence that He will make good things out of what we are facing.

No matter what you face, there are powerful tools at the heart and core of faith-filled people. You should know about these weapons and hang onto them for the most challenging times in life. These provide a fountain of power for your soul in the most troubling situations.

Romans 8:28 is my favorite gritty verse in our entire collection of letters from God. It says: We know that God causes everything to work together for the good of those who love Him and are called according to His purpose.

This concept is profound. No matter what you are going through, God is working for your good and causing everything else to do that too! He can turn every kind of life event into something that helps you and develops good for you! On the negative side, He can turn evil, mistakes, pain, and accidents into something useful in your life if you simply trust Him with them. On the positive side, even those can be turned into powerful tools if we put them in God's hands.

In John 10:10, Jesus adds gritty power to every believer through his declaration. While our enemy comes to "steal, kill, and destroy," Jesus came to help us live the great life, a life that is abundant in every way!

Some bleak and discouraging thinkers rob us with an inner belief that evil is stronger than good and that it will win in the end. They are wrong. It is the enemy who wants to steal long life from us, make us poor and inadequate, or destroy little pieces of happiness in our lives. All it really takes to live the great life is to truly trust God with it and allow Him room to build a gritty worldview that blows out the devil with the sheer force of faith.

And I want to add one more powerful, grit-building concept. In Genesis 12, God lists seven powerful blessings that he wants for every believer. Among them is this powerful statement: "I will make your name great."

God is comforting Abraham by telling him that it is his destiny to become famous! In other words, God wants you to know that the desire deep within you to matter and to make a difference comes from God and is His desire for you! Every believer has these powerful promises-- that no matter what you face, God will bring you out and bless you if you can simply trust Him with it! (See Galatians 3).

GRIT VALUES DIGNITY

Self-esteem is important, of course,. but how self-esteem is achieved is also important.

My opinion of myself means something, and the opinion of others also helps, but world changers have found something deeper. They find a cause that is bigger than themselves, which then makes their own lives bigger as well.

Gideon had an encounter with an angel. David had years of practice and winning against wild beasts before he came up against Goliath. Even then, he quoted confidence in His God and did not make exaggerated statements about his own power.

It is valuable to love yourself. But everything only has a value based on what someone was willing to pay for it. You are a creation of God and so valuable to Him that He gave the most valued thing He had to offer in exchange for your soul. You matter to Him.

A self-esteem built on how much God thinks of you, how much He cares for you, and how much He paid for you, gives dignity to every part of the human experience because it is a value set by our designer. This esteem that we choose for ourselves adds value to every decision in life and to every step we take toward becoming a persevering and powerful force for good.

Try this: Look in a mirror at yourself and say the Genesis 12 blessings over yourself; "God will make me into a great nation. He will bless me, and make me famous. I will be a blessing to others. God will bless those who bless me. He will curse those who treat me with contempt. All families on earth will be blessed because of me."

GETTING GRITTY: BELIEVING IN SOMETHING DEEPER

1. What steps do I need to take to "get smart" in my calling? What do I need to learn?

_____

_____

_____

2. Often the things we love and hate are connected to our purpose. What insights do I see here?

_____

_____

_____

3. Dignity matters. Is my self-esteem built on superficial things or on the way I conduct my life?

_____

_____

_____

Pray with me:

"God, help me develop my purpose with passion and move forward with the study, dignity, and faith I need to achieve my dreams."

Chapter 5
Grit is Constantly Learning and Adapting

"Our very survival depends on our ability to stay awake, to adjust to new ideas, to remain vigilant and to face the challenge of change."

--Martin Luther King, Jr.

I don't know how many times I've been to the Dominican Republic. At this point, it would be like expecting someone to accurately report the number of times they've been to the post office. It's too routine to pick out in my memory.

That's not to say my time spent in the DR

has been unmemorable. I remember very fondly the hand-painted murals in bright colors, the happy women performing lively worship dances, the straw-holes drilled into coconuts to drink the juice straight. And I remember the rough stuff, too--the first four or five trips almost entirely, for example, when we couldn't get things to fall together.

I was there with a team from Freedom Valley Church, answering a request from a church called Prince of Peace to help them reach their community with love, service, and teaching.

Four or five times, there were endless roadblocks. Sometimes literally, as roads are often made of dirt and (also pretty often) are long, treacherous, and lead you into the wilderness before abruptly stopping altogether, while the voice on the GPS assures you that the city you are seeking is somewhere up ahead.

And then there were other things, the kind that can occur anywhere in the world, like local politics, religious politics, and weather. And language-based misunderstandings. And technological failures. And illness. And taking your stuff with you everywhere because the locals swear up and down that leaving anything in your hotel while you're out will get it stolen fast.

It was rough for a while.

On the next trip, I took a large team of people. We had sent ahead some graphics and teaching materials in a computer file that we were told could be printed and distributed by the time we arrived. It didn't work out, but I'm getting ahead of myself.

After we had landed in the DR and deplaned, the bus we had arranged for picking up our big group didn't show. So we had to shrug it off and rent another one. By the time we finally arrived in Padre Las Casas, we found out about the flyers-- no printer. Not happening.

So we drove back to the capital, bought a printer, and started printing the flyers we needed for that night's teaching event. We reduced the size of the flyer so we could get four on a page, and then cut them. Our little printer started inching away, giving us excruciatingly few pages per minute, while my eager-to-work team waited like scissor-wielding vultures. I woke up every two hours all night to feed that little printer more pages so that we would have plenty the next day. The machine got so hot I thought parts inside it might start melting down.

When we would get a little stack going, the team would split up and frantically hand them out to anybody in town who would take them. We weren't going to let our weird, slow day keep us down.

The coolest part of this story is that, while the Prince of Peace church can comfortably contain 100 or maybe 150 people, almost 400 showed up. We were thrilled and quickly found ways of adding more seats and more ways of getting these people involved in our crazy little event.

The uncool part of the story is that, as I got the nod from the local pastor to get this exciting night started, the power went out.

In the entire town.

This isn't a rare thing, apparently, because the hardy church leaders quickly produced a generator, and my team threw their hands over their hearts in sweet, exhausted relief.

But the generator wouldn't keep running. Then it was discovered that the gas, recently replenished, had been stolen out of the generator's tank.

Not a problem, say the kind, quick-thinking locals. *We'll go get gas and be right back.*

They returned a while later with news that because of the power outage, the gas station was closed.

There's another one, but it's not very close. We'll go try that one.

The crowd began to melt away. We tried keeping their interest without power, but talking to 400 human beings who are each crammed against three or four other human beings, many of them children, was very difficult without an audio system.

The gas guys came back, with gas, and we got started with our service very, very late. Instead of the hundreds of people we could have originally prayed with and talked to, about eight people responded to our message.

I went to the back of the church feeling defeated.

I cried for my eager team, working so hard for so little. I sobbed for myself, exhausted and unsure of my abilities to lead them. I sobbed for the people of the Dominican Republic, especially those who had showed up and sacrificed their evening for a boring, annoying representation of the love we were trying to show them.

We tried a few other things with varying level of success, but nothing that felt like the home run we had come there for, the one that God and I had discussed at length. I knew there was more work to be done there, but it felt overwhelmingly difficult to proceed. A few days later on our way home, I wondered if it was worth it. It seemed bonkers to spend my time on something that was not very fruitful.

It seemed especially bonkers to return to the DR *again*.

I prayed about it endlessly. "Is this really something worth my time, God? Is this really worth the time, energy, and money of my team? Is it worth more embarrassment?" I could feel God nodding, ever patient with me as I made myself sound so important. *Yes. It is really worth it.*

So we went back a year later, more determined than ever. Instead of giving in to the fear of fruitlessness, we arranged to go bigger. Our next attempt was a large-scale festival for Padre Las Casas. We rented out a baseball field and invited the entire surrounding area to come learn about the principles of Jesus, allow us to pray for them, let us learn about the needs of their community, and help us come up with crazy, beautiful ways of showing them love.

And like the lightest, breeziest tidal wave, the masses poured in. Every afternoon into evening, we put up on that stage any talented musician, drama team, or public speaker that we could find. God worked through us, performing miraculous healings of some well-known people in that little town. By the end of our four-day event, we packed the stadium with thousands of people. We talked; they listened. They talked; we listened. And every church in town reported standing-room-only for a year following.

But I'm getting ahead of myself again.

Months after I returned from the most recent awful trip to the DR and months before the wonderful, stadium-packed trip to the DR, I was in Nepal.

My good friend Johannes Amritzer is a missionary who frequently draws crowds of thousands in foreign countries, where often the name of Jesus or the concept of divine love has never been heard before. He certainly doesn't draw the crowds because of celebrity--again, these are remote cities of sometimes impoverished people who would have no reason to know him-- but because he has a mysterious knack for attracting hoards. This was a knack I could really use, so I was there to hang out with him and learn from him.

GRIT ASKS FOR HELP

I didn't feel ready to hear great advice, even if he had it. I couldn't handle my 400-person crowd when I got that, so the concept of attracting thousands of people who speak another language and are probably skeptical of me didn't sound anything but scary and exhausting. But I asked for it anyway, because ready or not, God was trying to do something in the Dominican Republic, and I wanted to be part of it.

I asked him how to throw a successful festival in an impoverished city. His response was so simple and brilliant and obvious that I could hear bells ding-donging in my happy little brain.

"Pick a city where it's never been done before."

My mind back-flipped into our other trips to the DR. The Holy Spirit started connecting dots in my brain. We were trying these little meetings that had been done before. We had tried passing out flyers and responding to crises in ways that had been done before. Maybe our initial approach in the earliest stages, before even arriving in the country, had been all wrong. Maybe we were bored because we were being boring! Maybe God was waiting to give us the stadium until we were ready to hit it out of the park.

I knew that a large-scale festival had never been done in Padre Las Casas before. I knew it would be a big, fat deal if there were one. I knew it would excite the local people in a way that would open up their ears and hearts to receive the banner we'd been trying to wave, the one that said WE LOVE YOU LIKE SERIOUSLY A LOT.

It didn't make sense to try *anything* in the DR again, let alone something bigger, more expensive, and requiring an even bigger team. I got some looks from my staff at Freedom Valley that said "Uh, everything we've tried there has failed. So maybe no?"

GRIT ANSWERS TO GOD

I had to trust that God was up to something, and I had to have faith that He would renew the energy of my team, too. There were times when we sought other missions organizations for help, and they turned us down. I could feel God saying to me, "Well, I didn't tell those organizations to do this. I told *you* to do this."

We went for the dream, and we got it. My gritty Freedom Valley people gave their time, energy, prayers, and money, and we went and got it done. We rallied around a goal with everything we had. We committed to learning anywhere we could, adapting anywhere we needed to, and we got it done. It's been my honor and privilege to continue returning to the DR, helping the local churches welcome their new, large congregations, and showing them love.

GRIT BRAVES THE UNKNOWN

The grit God is showing us in the Dominican Republic still has purpose in the future. Helping others is a core principle of Jesus. Sometimes reaching out to other cultures reveals issues in our own culture. Sometimes it's just good for the soul. Sometimes they have a lot to teach *us*. And often, it's good practice for a large group of comparatively-wealthy Americans to remind other parts of the world that we want to love them. Our dream includes filled churches here as well as there.

It's scary to try new things, but I encourage you to step into the unknown and all the vulnerability that comes with it. God didn't ask someone else to do it; he asked *you* to do it.

GETTING GRITTY: LEARNING AND ADAPTING

1. Are there mere obstacles in my life that I've labeled as dead ends?

_____

_____

_____

2. Who can I ask for help and advice?

_____

_____

_____

3. Are there areas of my quest where I'm thinking too small?

_____

_____

_____

Pray with me:

"God, help me to learn and adapt as I go. Keep me from stubbornness and doubt. I trust you."

Chapter 6
Grit Has Partnership

"I am a success today because I had a friend who believed in me, and I didn't have the heart to let him down."

--Abraham Lincoln

Jonathan was the son of the king of Israel, which naturally put him in line for the throne. He had a lot going for him and a bright future.

Except for one thing. He was the son of a king who could not get it together and who was losing his kingdom because he tended to give in to fear in tense moments.

Like right now. The Philistines were hovering over them. They held the high ground, and their armies outnumbered Israel. The Philistines glittered with sharp technology that the few fighting men left with King Saul did not have, and the Israelites were left hiding wherever they could.

But Jonathan added things up differently than his father. One day Jonathan said to his armor bearer "Come on, let's go over to the Philistine outpost."

Not one single thing seems to be known about that armor bearer except his gritty response. When Jonathan suggested that just the two of them should start an attack, from which it was very likely that they would never return, the armor bearer answered, "Go ahead, I am with you heart and soul."

When circumstances get rough and your life is at stake, it is an amazing gift to have someone with you who is also willing to risk it all in the fight of your life. Every fruitful leader needs an armor bearer like Jonathan had that day.

GRIT PARTNERS UP

These two guys started a fight against an entire army and won the day. None of it was easy. None of it came from a "if it was meant to be, it will be" attitude. They climbed a cliff to face their first attacker. Somehow, they won. Another one came at them. Eventually they got him too. But after two huge victories, there were still thousands of soldiers ahead of them! Logically, how could they ever hold a sword long enough to win against thousands of them? There were so many reasons to believe this grit would get them killed.

I Samuel 14 tells us that this went on for quite a while until they had killed about twenty of the bad guys and panic started breaking out among the enemy. Then they finally got help from their own army, who had been hiding, and later even the weather started helping. In other words, these two little Hebrew men, all by themselves, had boldly put themselves out there a long time before winning even looked remotely possible.

Deuteronomy 32:30 suggests that any one of us can put 1,000 of the enemy to flight, but, if we believe, any two of can chase away up to 10,000!

That's an outrageous, audacious belief in our ability to change the world together. Moses does curious war math, doesn't he?

Similarly however, Jesus told us, "Where two or three agree as touching anything, it will be done for them!" In other words, whether in physical battle or in spiritual battle, partnerships matter to God, and they add strength exponentially. He seems to get even more interested when two or more agree on a thing.

I think this statement that Jesus made has stunning implications. It might be one of His most provocative assertions. God will subject Himself in some sense to anything two or three people agree together on? This is amazing stuff!

It really seems harder than one might think to get two people to agree on anything. But when we do achieve this powerful melding of minds, God responds to it in amazing ways, even declaring that they will indeed have His help, and that He will multiply their outcomes far beyond the sum of their parts.

When I was a little boy growing up on a Beachy-Amish farm, my dad took me to a horse-pulling event. We watched horses pulling heavy things for hours. For my dad, this was great fun.

And while horses didn't blow my skirt up the way they did for others, I remember learning something pretty cool about them from my dad on that day.

"When one horse is pulling on its own, it can pull maybe as much as 8,000 pounds. You'd think that when two horses pull together, they can pull twice as much, 16,000. But they can pull three times as much! Two horses working together are stronger than the sum of their parts." I never saw Dad's theory actually proven, but it was clear he believed it, and it stuck in my head.

I've personally seen the power of friendship so many times.

I was lucky to have a friend in school named Mel Beiler. He is still one of my closest friends and motorcycle-riding buddies. We were in third grade together in our little Amish-Mennonite schoolhouse. As we got older, we leaned on each other when we made decisions, and having him in my life kept me from making countless dumb mistakes in my youth. And probably a few more recently.

I've learned and relearned this concept in my life.

When Freedom Valley Church was starting up, I went to a pastor's training conference where the speaker warned us just-starting-out pastors to not go it alone. He said that pastors who start churches alone rarely make it, because when the hard days come (and they come early and often), there's nobody to lean on, nobody to remind them why they wanted to do this. And they bail.

I drove home from that conference praying, "God, I need a partner in this. I know I can't do it alone. I need somebody to take the pressure off my wife, to pick up all the slack, somebody who thinks about church all the time, somebody who wants to start a great one with me. Who can I ask to help me?"

And then it occurred to me--Marvin Stanley.

Marvin was a friend of mine who was in his senior year at Valley Forge Christian College. He was not interested at all in coming to Gettysburg, at all, ever. But I asked if he would just come out to visit. He did. He still was not interested. He said kind things, but ultimately turned me down again.

After he graduated I called him to check in and see how things were going (and to shamelessly slip in another request to come help me).

He said he was thinking about Gettysburg. Seriously. What's more, he was willing to take on the parts of the job I was really, really bad at, like organization and planning and anything else involving administration.

Marvin's first year as a pastor at Freedom Valley Church was the best year to date, and we enjoyed a hardworking-but-fruitful partnership as attendance went up, involvement went up, and people started to mysteriously dig our place of worship. We straightened each other out, kept each other on our toes, and to this day, he's one of the strongest pillars in our operation. While I am a visionary, he is a master strategist. I am good at recruiting and helping leaders see their potential. He is good at helping them develop their potential. I feel like I value his friendship more now than ever.

We could pull more weight together than the sum of our parts.

GRIT HONESTLY ASSESSES ITS SKILLSET

Jesus sent out the disciples in pairs. Moses had Aaron (and later Joshua), Barnabas had Paul. Paul had Silas, and at times others. The Bible is full of the power of partnerships. Strong, gritty people are often people who have certain skills, but they know they need other skills as well to get the job done. Truly, Freedom Valley's achievements are as much or more a result of Marvin's skills than because of mine.

Maybe you too have a desire to get something significant done. Perhaps your first step could be to find a partner, someone who will go to battle with you even if it has the potential to cost them their very lives.

If you can find a partner, perhaps you can find the grit that will change the world. Gritty leaders seek a partner and can't stop sharing their vision until somebody comes back with "I am with you heart and soul," like Jonathan's armor bearer.

GRIT CAN BE SURPRISING

There are people around you right now who

wish to be involved in something worth giving themselves to. Their calling is to help you develop your calling. Their heart's desire is to partner with someone whose calling and gifts can multiply their own calling and gifts.

Of course, partnerships can be hard, too. There are times when Marvin and I don't see eye to eye, or just plain don't get each other. To keep any goal alive, you need allies, but to keep allies, sometimes you have to be flexible within your goal. It's here again where the power of kindness and empathy are invaluable. Sometimes we have to remind ourselves that life is full of seasons, and a partner may only be called to help us through a particular season.

Whatever the particulars of your quest, I pray that God blesses you with a partner in your calling.

GETTING GRITTY: PARTNERSHIP

1. What am I great at? What's my God-given skill set?

_____

_____

2. In what areas of skill am I lacking?

_____

_____

_____

3. What kind of partner do I need to accomplish my vision? Do I know that person, or do I need to ask God for an ally?

_____

_____

_____

Pray with me:

> "God, send me an ally. Help me to be a good friend to those who are rooting for me. Show me what my strengths are."

Chapter 7
Grit Has Boundaries and Self-Control

"Those who disregard discipline despise themselves, but the one who heeds correction gains understanding."

--Proverbs 15:32

Gritty people are people of self-control.

People who get things done have a way of lashing themselves to a goal so tightly that they don't have time, energy, or interest in the things that will get them off track. The very passion for particular achievements keeps them self-

controlled because they believe that any lack of
self-control has the real potential of locking them
outside the possibility of achieving the desired
outcome.

Self-control is best sustained when one has
built a passionate goal and now will do whatever
it takes to achieve the goal, however improbable
that goal might seem.

How many of our illnesses come from the
inability to discipline oneself with a simple day off
every week? The Bible stresses the need for that
day off on the same list of top-ten boundaries as
the command against murder. Obviously this
particular measure of self-control is serious to
God. Our bodies need the time to heal
themselves. People who have serious goals that
take decades to accomplish will make sure that
this rest time happens, or they will pay the price
with sicknesses.

To the gritty, self-control is about staying
focused on a visionary goal. It is not so much
about staying self-controlled just for its own sake.
The energy for it comes from a deep conviction
that every kind of sin is only a prohibition against
that which would destroy our abilities. There are
no random orders not to do things in God's
economy. All of His statements of self-control

are about adding value to my life and keeping
self-induced obstacles out of my way. "Sins"
could also be called "self-destructive habits." It
makes sense that a loving Father would
encourage us to stay away from them.

The grit to keep going when the going gets
tough is buoyed by a passionate, self-motivated
self-discipline and a love for any knowledge that
keeps me out of trouble. It is driven by a hunger
to avoid the kinds of habits that inhibit my ability
to stay in the flow of productivity towards my
glowing goal. Then the good habits I've picked
up help me enjoy the fruits of my labor on the
other side of success.

The entanglements of what we call "sin" are
prohibited so we can avoid what would steal joy
from us or dampen our happiness. Smart people
constantly collect the motivation that it takes to
live a life where regrets will be few in the long
run, and every opportunity to win is maximized.

The former-shepherd-boy-turned-king,
David, declared that he loved God's law, not
seeing it as a "prohibition against all fun" as
society sometimes calls it, but viewing God's law
as the secret to sustained happiness and
effectiveness. Therefore it is a treasured secret

and a highly valued skill. As such, it must be honed, admired, protected, and grown.

I love your instructions! I think about them all day long. Your commands make me wiser than my enemies, for they are my constant guide....How sweet your words taste to me; they are sweeter than honey. Your commandments give me understanding. (Psalm 119)

David was not indulging in resentful jokes about God's commands. David was loving God's commands because they saved him pain and helped him build a great life.

To hate the rules is to hate life and to hate winning in life. But these rules are not best imposed on others. They are about self-discipline. They are ways that I measure my own heart's ability to focus on achieving the calling God put on my life, and they provide me with the ability to sustain focus for the long haul.

All of the other items on God's Top Ten boundaries, otherwise known as the Ten Commandments, build the same case. Look at them like this:

1. Thou shalt have no other Gods before me.

In other words: Decide who you are by deciding who you will obey. Obey God. When you're not sure what to do, pray to God and do what you feel in your spirit to be right, even if it doesn't make sense to others. It's the policy that won't leave you filled with regrets.

2. Thou shalt not make unto thee any graven image.

In other words: Guard your affections. Don't let your heart get attached to anything else higher than honoring God with your life, which means following your purpose, which means doing what you do best, which means living a full, joyful life.

3. Thou shalt not take the name of the Lord thy God in vain.

In other words: Blame evil for evil. Don't get mad at God for what God did not do. And don't say "God told me" to manipulate people.

4. Remember the Sabbath day, to keep it holy.

In other words: Take a full day off every week. You need it. Take it seriously. It's healthy for you, your family, and the quality of your work.

5. Honor thy father and thy mother.

In other words: You have to be real about who you are and where you came from, and find value there.

6. Thou shalt not kill.

In other words: Murder is not an option. It causes more pain than solution.

7. Thou shalt not commit adultery.

In other words: Adultery is stupid. It will hurt everybody around you.

8. Thou shalt not steal.

In other words: Earn your stuff.

9. Thou shalt not bear false witness against thy neighbor.

In other words: Lying about people will catch up with you.

10. Thou shalt not covet.

In other words: Don't let your heart fantasize about your neighbor's wife, house, land or anything else. It will make a mess of your priorities and your judgment.

I don't mean these to be oversimplifications of the powerful ten commandments. But you can see that these rules are not fun-stealers. They are life-givers. Breaking one of them can rob a person of the ability to function at all, or erode one's ability to achieve the things he once dreamed of getting done.

GRIT VALUES GUIDEPOSTS

Gritty people are not afraid of the structure of rules. They accept a level of meaning that comes from life's define-ability, and they embrace the clarity of disciplined skills, boundaries that can be clearly enumerated and purposefully scored. They get that God's rules are clues that lead to real joy in life.

And while there is a value to rules, and boundaries add meaning to achievements and relationships, it is self-control that trumps all other kinds of controls for those who aspire to gritty achievements. The quality of being able to control yourself is central to the person who wishes to make it across the finish line. Certainly this is why the Holy Spirit included a *lot* about self-control in the Bible.

The former-death-squad-leader-turned-apostle, Paul, reassured us that self-control is always possible! In 1 Corinthians 10:13 he asserts that we will never be tempted beyond our ability to resist. So, no food can overpower you, no sexual temptation is irresistible, and no urge to envy can make us do anything. His brother, apostle James, made an even more pointed observation that we are responsible for the ability to be deceived because we are only deceived by our own lusts. Therefore, even deceit is my own responsibility and is preventable by self-control.

GRIT IS HUMBLE

When I am not in self-control, my own control urge seems to project outside of me, criticizing others and all of their choices. If I am not eating healthy, I suddenly find myself feeling critical toward everyone else's choices in food. If I am not exercising, I find myself critical of anyone else who is not paying attention to their health.

Every spring, for example, as we start shedding the extra clothing, someone comes to me to protest how the women of the church dress too provocatively. And while women should dress mindfully, there is no modesty sufficient to keep an undisciplined mind from wandering. As a little Amish boy growing up in the Amish culture, where women virtually dress in sacks, even this did not stop me from having a mind that needed serious discipline to keep it from lusting. And how I was struggling with lust inside was evidenced when I was the most critical of others and how they dressed.

Jesus taught that adultery would never become a physical temptation until it had become settled in the mind (Matthew 5:27-28), so we should understand that adultery really originally happens in the heart. And it is in the heart that self-discipline counts most because if thoughts are controlled, actions are fairly easy to control.

Anyone who is really and truly practicing self-control of their thoughts is humbled by the very attempt to be in self-control. It is a humiliating and constant strain on one's pride to admit how much work we really have to do to maintain the walls of the Holy City inside ourselves. Those who really manage to do so are humbled enough to stay soft and tender toward others who might be struggling with it or have given in completely.

And the temptation to jump to judgment should be a red flag inside that I am out of order in some way with my own thoughts, because if I were seriously controlling my own thoughts, my pride would be broken by my own humiliating failures; my joy would be boundless that God in His grace allows my shortcomings to stay hidden.

There are no foes unconquered if we stay in a humble, honest place before God. Otherwise, God Himself becomes the foe and resists the proud. When I am in pride (James 4:6) there is no one to appeal to, to remove that particular obstacle. The only way to return to God's favor is to humble oneself again, returning to a place where the favor of God is upon us because "He gives favor to the humble."

GRIT SEEKS DISCIPLINE

Ryan Wade recently came into my life through an episode of humbling himself before God and people. His story, from childhood, is a story with amazing grit. As a young boy, his mother was involved in a serious car accident, and shortly after that he and his brother were placed in foster care. He felt punished and angry inside about what he had to face and the adjustments he had to make.

As a young man he got involved in criminal activity and was caught and sent to prison. When he got out, he found that his only recourse was living in a tent in the woods. One day police told him he had to move--and he felt thrown out of his homelessness.

One day he wandered into Central Assembly of God in Cumberland, Maryland, where an astute youth pastor saw a certain brokenness and invited him to talk. That pastor introduced Ryan to Jesus and eventually got him started with an organization called Teen Challenge to get a fresh start. It was an exhilarating new life, but after getting a few principles in place, he felt he had life under control and left the program early.

But the same evil that got Ryan involved in self-destructive behaviors then constantly spoke in his ear about how dumb it was to leave Teen Challenge early and told him that life was hopeless. Ryan did his best to labor under it, even showing some amazing grit by turning himself in for past bench warrants and serving time.

But while in Adam's County Adult Correctional complex, Ryan found a pamphlet about the Freedom House, our church's ministry to people who want to start a whole new life. He took a deep breath and humbled himself to reach out for help. He wanted to lead a great life when he got out, to make a profound and lasting change, and he was looking for help to do it.

Ryan did it. Humbling himself to receive help removed more barriers and ended up putting him near a wonderful, Godly woman for him to marry. Together they are planning for and building a great life and a great future. Gritty faith drove Ryan to reach out and try something that would humble him and drive faith even deeper. I consider him an amazing man of God on the way to a wonderful future.

Persevering, overcoming followers of Jesus do not have time to be out of control or to laugh about the lack of personal discretion. They have a job to do, and they consider any outside distraction a waste of their valuable time.

GETTING GRITTY: BOUNDARIES

1. What areas of my life need discipline?

_____

_____

Pray with me:

"God, help me to humbly seek instruction where I need it."

Chapter 8
Grit Is Passionate

"The passionate commitment of the LORD of Heaven's Armies will make this happen!"
--Isaiah 37:32b

"The two most important days in your life are the day you were born, and the day you find out why."
--Mark Twain

If self-control is the protection of the dream, passion is its heart and energy. The prophet Isaiah declares that it is God's passion that will make the improbable happen and will cause His people to eventually break through.

Zeal, or sustained enthusiasm, does not generate itself. Anyone who wishes to achieve anything of value continually builds, maintains, and nurtures this vital ingredient of the heart. Paul links it to laziness by saying, "Never be lazy, but work hard and serve the Lord enthusiastically."

The power to make it through the tough times in life is directly connected to the ability to motivate oneself or to maintain enthusiasm. At a family get-together recently, one family member guardedly asked me if I ever struggle with enthusiasm for my work, and assuming that I did, how do I maintain it?

One businessman told me that he doesn't even try to maintain enthusiasm. He told me that the longest that he can maintain enthusiasm for anything is about ten years. He gets started with something, begins to build it, and then a few years into it hits his stride. By year six or seven, it is typically going well, because he is a gifted leader and can do almost anything. By year eight or nine, he is struggling to be interested at all and usually ends up walking away and doing something else.

While this works for him, many of us are called to things that will take decades to accomplish. We simply cannot afford to walk away from something after ten years, because our calling cannot be accomplished in such a short time.

For us, then, the primary need is to build and maintain zeal or enthusiasm for the things that we have been called to do. It is up to us to find the motivation inside to not only keep doing it, but also to keep our interest piqued and passions high.

Leaders have to do this for their teams. While it can feel daunting, it is very much part of a leader's job to keep up enthusiasm for their team. Otherwise, the team burns out. Guess what—for your calling, your dream—you're the leader! It's your job to keep up your own enthusiasm so *you* don't burn out.

So, what is helpful in keeping our passions high for the one thing God has called us to do? I'd like to suggest a few things to try.

Inspiration. I find that my enthusiasm is renewed by fresh creativities. Foraging for new ideas and insights into my area of calling helps. Time spent reading, hearing the ideas of others, and prayer, often cause me to see things I might have missed and get excited about progress again. I've heard it said that great writers are great readers. I imagine that's true with every profession. Take the time to see what others in your field are up to--if it's writing, read what others have written. If it's farming, see what other farmers are trying. If it's drinking coffee while standing on your head, find somebody else who loves to do that and get some pointers!

Rest. When I am struggling with motivation for what God has called me to do, I often need to check my rest schedule. Taking that full day off every week is rejuvenating to my soul and often unlocks enthusiasm for the things I have been called to. Even further, the Bible suggests that every seven years more rest is needed, perhaps an extended vacation. An extended sabbatical of rest every seventh year gives leaders support to take extra time to get inner rejuvenation and to rest enough to sustain the journey ahead enthusiastically. Long-range perseverance cannot happen without rhythms of rest being built and practiced.

Last summer, Mel Beiler and Merrill Smucker asked if I would be interested in an extended motorcycle ride with them. I wasn't sure I really needed a break, but these two guys are deeply encouraging and giving to me and have been so for the past thirty-five years. I had a sabbatical coming, and finally I said I'd do it.

We took off across the country, stopping by Omar Beiler's place (a mentor of mine) in the Midwest. He rode south with us into Arkansas for a great day of beautiful sunshine and seeing the sights of the heartland. I find my motorcycle an amazing place to pray, reflect, plan, and just think.

On our third or fourth day of riding, I started noticing something that was happening to me. I enjoyed riding at the back of the pack, and *not* being involved in any decisions. I started realizing that most days in ministry I am agonizing about decisions that I have to make, and that while riding along with several trusted friends, I could just not make decisions for a while.

Somewhere on about day number three, I even asked Mel if he would lead for days in a row, allowing me to just troll along in the back of the group, not even chiming in for decisions about where to eat, where to sleep, or what roads to take--at all! He graciously agreed, and for days I just…rested. They discussed traveling south to Albuquerque then north along the Rockies till we got to Yellowstone. I felt like they decided these things while I nodded numbly to whatever, for days.

Gratitude. It was an amazing time! On that ride I consciously tried to limit my prayer requests for a while and just be thankful, just breathe, just enjoy the moment. Day after day I found my breathing get deeper, my courage feel stronger, my enthusiasm for life--even the challenges I saw ahead--feel easier to overcome. Gratitude is a powerful magnet for attracting joy and passion.

When I finally got back, several staff members said I was exhibiting some amazing energy and excitement. For everything! I felt it flowing out of me again, easily. Hugging people, loving my critics, being there for those that I could, all just felt like it was in me in an easy abundance. And last evening I called Mel to say we need to schedule another long ride, because it was worth it to rest deeply and get to that place again.

As I get older, I do understand more and more how important rest is for a personality like mine. I often put so much pressure on myself: I expect that there should be more rest, more Bible reading, more prayer, more reaching my neighbors, more time spent preparing messages, more churches, more leaders trained, more time spent with those who are hurting, more time spent with my family, more time spent writing, and more giving. You get it. You probably have your own list.

And while I am the first to protest that "I am not that tired!," and that I don't need or want more time off, I have been the beneficiary of mentors and friends who have encouraged me to take it anyway, and I have benefitted deeply for doing it.

Celebration. If I am not so good at resting, I am even worse at another skill needed to sustain grit. That skill is celebrating the wins along the way.

Gritty people are quick to gain strength for the future by celebrating the wins that God has already given. The great leader Moses, when preparing his people for the battles ahead, reminded them to look back and celebrate what God had already done. When I take time to remember, celebrate, and enjoy what God has done, it becomes easier to face whatever challenges are ahead.

Leaders by their very nature tend to keep their eyes on the horizon and always be pressing toward the goal. That is their strength. But it can also be their weakness. No one can sustain energy for the long haul without taking time to celebrate the wins that have already been given. When I take the time to enjoy what God has done, the capillaries of my vision open up to allow Him to do it again, and to enjoy the moments when He does.

If it feels like little progress has been made lately, maybe it's because we have not celebrated what God has already given! I cannot see His movements well enough when I am restlessly pushing ahead and not acknowledging each blessing and each fortunate step into pleasant wins while they happen..

The ability to persevere is in itself an incredible gift from God. To treasure it is to build it. To build it is to break through. And to break through creates permanent vistas of opportunity that can only be experienced by someone who hung on to belief when and where others chose not to.

So here's to the Gritty! I pray that you are already one of them, or will become one. I pray that your grit will see you through.

ACKNOWLEDGEMENTS

I want to thank Sally, Janice, Charity, and my wife, Julie, for their invaluable input on this book. I would also like to thank my daughter, Shawna, for editing.

25887211R00071

Made in the USA
Charleston, SC
17 January 2014

THE GRIT PROJECT

ingredients of perseverance

by Gerry Stoltzfoos

Edited by Shawna Stoltzfoos